Fragments of Verbiage

A Book Of Poems

Nikki M. Robinson-Williams

iUniverse, Inc.
New York   Bloomington

Fragments of Verbiage
A Book Of Poems

iUniverse books may be ordered through booksellers or by contacting:

iUniverse
1663 Liberty Drive
Bloomington, IN 47403
www.iuniverse.com
1-800-Authors (1-800-288-4677)

ISBN: 978-1-4401-8281-5 (pbk)
ISBN: 978-1-4401-8283-9 (cloth)
ISBN: 978-1-4401-8282-2 (ebk)

Printed in the United States of America

iUniverse rev. date: 10/23/2009

I would like to thank J. Penski and D. Persons for Prior contributions on 'S.O.M.A.'
NMRW

This is for the colors
This is for the 90 degree angles once again squared
Surrounded by many and plenty of paisleys
My dew my do that which I do
And the rags that hang from this hand
This is for the carpal tunnel
That burns within the same
This is for the mothers that should be embracing you
The fathers that should be relieving you of your pains
This is for the Made in Paris feeling we want to believe in
It doesn't matter what you are
When you feel displaced
With no one to blame
Anyone other than yourself
Perhaps it wasn't you

This is documented on the edge of the ceilings of our minds
My dew my do that which I do
And the rags that sit on my head
This is for all the hemorrhaging in my legs my hands
For this thing I call love
Protect yourself
Love yourself
Heal yourself
So you in turn you can do the same
For someone else

This is for the few that exist and do
And the many that say not all feel the same
In that of the free where who is made

For A.R., the children & to the Moaning Children

Applause to Freedom…

Love,

Speech

Have a bit of tea with me
I said have a bit of tea with me
Get your mug or your cup
Fill it up
Fill it up
Add a bag of Comment Constants
The Naranja & Negro solamente por favor
Before you submerge it
Take it close
Inhale the orange scent
And exhale your troubles freely
Now dip
Let it sit
Let it sit
And have a cup of tea with me
I said have a cup of tea with me
Sit back with your throw
Hopefully it is your favorite quilt
And get warm and cozy with me
I said get warm and cozy with me
Read a bit
Sip a bit
Sip a bit
Read a bit
And set your mind adrift the sea
Set your mind adrift the sea
Come on and have that cup of tea with me
And take it all
Easy
…Until your cup is empty

Fragments of Verbiage

G

If I say I'll talk to you later
Will you talk to me
And if you do
Will you listen
For if you listen
You will understand
And I will
And we will
Each other
For if you are my friend
You will
And if I say you are a friend
Then that is which you are
And you will always be
Even if
You don't feel the same for me

For that I adore you
As a friend
And forever will
And you'll not expect that of me
G

It will hail
And we will be
Yes, it will extend as a heat wave
And we will be
And it will never end
My G

~ 1991 ~

For G & R

Was Not

Was not going to jump in
In someone's cama no sutra
Bed I know
Know nothing more than
The unmentioned adored

And they quietly said
She is of that type
She is of that type
For sure

Was not going to give my life
Life for something
Something I've already seen
Seen that road
Road of falsities
Dreams of failed love
Love and unions

And they quietly said
She is of that type
She is of that type
For sure

Was not the one to give him time
Time to love
Love again and break my heart
Heart broken many a time
Time when…. Where has Reality gone?

And they quietly said
She is of that type
That type for sure
How far from the truth,
So far from pure

Listening Anymore

Early in the morning
Some sunny days
Mommy and Daddy are going their way
As they walk out the door
There's something I wish to yell
But I wait

Late noon
No one to turn to
They say bomb threats at school
A fourteen year old pregnant
Happy it's not me
I'm young
I'm free
Something I want to say
I wait

Standing in front of the micro
Looking a the stove
Heating last weeks leftovers
Feeling a little cold
Sitting near the TV
Searching for company
Music is for me
I've something to say
Yet I wait

Walking in a daze
To strong discussion
Seeming a little heated
It's very late
Daddy's leaving today
Something on my mind
I'll wait no more

How would I show it to my family
It all seems scary
But I won't
I can't
For it is too late

Something I've to say
I waited long enough
There's no meaning of love
They are not listening anymore
And I refuse to sit in dire straits

Mom has locked herself in her room
The locks changed on the door
And Dad's on the other side
Their love no more
They are not listening anymore
And I between one lock to next
And a wooden seam
There was something I wanted to say
And it is too late

I Want Your Heartache

I want your heartache
I want to know
Want to go
Where you've been
Where you are
Want to be more
Than your friend

Want to be the metacarpals of your hand
The marrow of your bones
I want to know your heartache
Not via phone

I want to have your lips to kiss
Your feet to caress
Your eyes to glare
Your heart to clear the naked mess

I want your heartache
Because they say that I am dying
Dying from a love
That now has consumed me

I want to be the trachea
Of your digestive system
The diaphragm of your respiratory
The lymph nodes that fight your pains
And if you let me
I'll make love to your brain

I want your heartache Baby
Don't think I can refrain
It's overwhelming
But well worth the strain

Where you are going
Let me be there
Let me see the rain

I want to know where
You are going
If you see
How I complain
And if you let me
I'll make love to your brain

I have to know if you are proud
If our love has been maintained
If I have done things
'Seemingly still the wrong way'
And as always
I'll give you my best
When I love you without constraints

Fragments of Verbiage

The baby now walking
Now running in the right life
Knowing nothing
But her first words
The mother looking on
Teaching Verbiage to be polite

Fragments from her mouth
Unfold
Verbiage has been told
To cover her mouth
As she burps towards the
Unsatisfied

Mon child
Notre pains
Mon birth
Notre gains
Say What?
Mon life
Mon stretch marks
Notre headaches
I willingly drained
For verbiage

For her I will not stop
For Verbiage
Her learning tools
Everywhere dropped
For utterance
Verbiage's cousin
For teachers
That fail to listen
And so quickly forget
For Verbiage

They think a blue pill,
Suffice it will
To Keep her attention twice
When by whose standards
We rate this child's
Attention to matter
For the unknown to evaluate
Or Verbiage to sit agape

Notre child
Mon womb
Mon courage
Given soon
Through her birth
To her
In her fragments understood

As her Father looks on concerned
Her Sister knows her every word
Her Brother writing on cognitive wood
That attempts to stand in her way
To break her existence
Yet it is the fragments intense
The words immense
That let me know Verbiage
Needs to commence
Her development of continuity
And Now Continuity Begins

Continuity

And I Sat

And I sat
Drinking the lonely man's tea
Wondering if this was meant to be
Am I meant to always be alone
I believe I have mistaken
It for independence
Hearing no ringer on the phone
I sit and wait
I contemplate
Have I ran true lovers away
Nothing could have been adequate
Everything was not good enough
Not love, not time
Not sweet nor divine
As I see no company
Coming my way
Strangely
There is no dismay

[Hidden]

What Were You

What were you
Coward like the poem
Hidden truth
Hidden lie
Down low on
Your down low high
They match it
Will they tell
Like fingerprints
On a Master
You possibly thought to target

Hear the pain
Seek your wisdom
I pray for peace
Where your
Confusion takes place
What were you
Hidden like this poem
Cowardliness
Cowardly
Coward
When M. Riddle shall confess

I'm like your
Last breath
You breathe
Upon her breast
Cowardly
Coward
Attempting to understand
Your pain
What are you then?
If we are not cowards like
This poem

Another Train

Another train rides to intrusions
Another tack of illusion
A conductor nowhere to be found
I thought I was homeward bound
But the fog blinding
Too confused
All to allude
My heart
As she was just a piece
A victim as a prize
He didn't care if he
Would trash her mind
Attempt to desecrate her soul
Attempt to embellish her
With holes as a moth
Would to clothes
In a closet left untouched
All on another train ride to confusion
This time her heart cries from contusions
And she will never love again
Yet only alone

One Adolescent Left Behind

I say that it was learned from your father
Your mother
Or one of your other care givers primary
You learned so well
You learned how to bully
There was no time spent to nurture you
To read to you
To hold you
Mold you into what you truly needed
Just one adolescent left behind

You managed to pick it up from
The lines between the bickering
You heard him say to her
That her worth was far from stellar
You heard her retort in all the pain
She felt within
You were one adolescent left behind

While your pain leaked again
From all the words she said to you
In frustration
She told you you were the replica
Of your father
It angered her everyday to see the man
She often despised
You learned it all too well
And you never really tried
Now you have to learn
To leave it all behind
If not
You will pass it right to
The children you have
Planted on this earth
Now all the bullying

The bully words
The aggression you have inside
Will have to stay
With that one adolescent
Left behind

Replica 2

And all this time
I thought I had to grow
Grow to know
This person inside
My parents now separated
Have shown me a new way
When I see her
I become the replica of him
When I see him
I the replica of she
Why don't they love me
For me
Why don't they see me
For the person
I have grown to be

And all this time
I thought I held my own
As me
They attempt to make
Replica, 2 of me
They will never see me
Individually as the me
That I am
They are too busy
Making the replica of me
They only see two of me
For when she sees my eyes
She sees the anger in his
When he sees my smile
He sees that he misses
The lips he use to kiss affectionately
Are just replicas to see

And So Quickly Forget

I'll take a bonus
I'll take more pay
I'll take the easy road any day
And quickly forget
What The Tree said
And quickly think the
Mis education understated in song
Was suppose to be
Rule of education well made
Teacher will you teach
What some so Quickly Forget

Teacher will you teach
What some so quickly forget
The child that came today
Not well nourished
The child that came today
From the unstable environment
The child that came today
Abused by the muse that sits at home
Will you add the fuel to write
His or her name in the concrete stone
Teacher will you teach
What some so quickly forget

You did it
When you yelled today
You did it
When you told that child
They won't matter anyway
You it you did it
With that sneer
You did it
All too well

Teacher will you teach
What some so quickly forget
Are you trying to meet
The demands never met
When you abruptly pull
The life of a child
In a scream meant for the dog
In your backyard
But you seem to treat the dog
Better than that child
Teacher will you teach
What some so quickly forget

What some forgot was drive
You became the one without spirit
What some forgot was fervor
You became the dead
What some forgot was ED 101
And the lesson plan became unread
Some forgot that one might be a bit advanced
And called him dumb instead
You are the teacher
The guidance counselor
That took the lazy/easy route
Instead

Untitled

I left you behind
Picked up my luggage
Got on that train
Rode straight through the land
On that railroad's track

I must have missed my ascension
Though it was only a few hours after slumber
That I saw the clouds unfold
I saw the sun take hold
Of my spirit
Gently
As I were a newborn
Kissing it tenderly
As if to caress

I saw that light of guide
Smiled
I was willing
I am not moving
I am paralyzed
I am submitting
That is
Myself
To the calmness of the air

No
You've called me
You are my voice
You don't want me
To completely ascend
So I come back
To your hollow call
And my spirit
Returns to my physical being
And I continue my journey
On life's train of diversity
Where will this end?

| 1991 |

Tears of Termination II

I lurked around and cried the tears of termination
The same tears I cried last year
The same ones to be disposed of next year
Tears cried years ago
And hence so
Years to come
The question I ask
Is why must love break so wrong
So sporadically
Unbelievably
The answers
Will never come
And I will continue
To cry the tears of termination
And no one will come
To mend my heart
To rid the hurt
To make me smile
That tear of termination
Will always leave a scar
So leak
Flow
Trickle if you must
For the tears of termination
I cry
Must not be thought as love
I will cry for trust

| 1991 |

Window of Paine

Look in the window Paine
See your reflection come through
Look in the window Paine
She always loved you
As the glass falls down
Will you remain standing
This is a reflection
Without Payne
No longer demanding
Now he's looking through
The window made of pain

20's

I don't need to be legal
For I would find nothing regal
About the case of being certified
For a drink in action
For I realize
The 20s have come upon me
If I think I know all
I am even besides myself
For the 20's have come
For me to add them to my shelf
And here I stand
Raising a champagne glass of
Sparkling Apple Cider
Thanking God for the knowledge
He's given me
I am still young
I've still to learn
And I've much more to consume
As the twenty's are no longer
Carefree

Realizing

Never realizing as much
What it is we take
The modest amount
We put back in
That which
We call create
And still there is so much
We put in reverse
With such young minds
We watch the news
To tell children
Peace is so hard to find

No Longer

No longer the questions rise
I now can answer them myself
The words no longer
Just fragments once formed
The fragments of verbiage
Running straight from my hold
Embrace her as she will know hope
Here it rises
Higher than any high riser
That may confine me
I see iniquity
Equality
Tranquillity
No boundaries found herein
No boundaries found therein

When You Look

I'll say it every time
When you look
Make sure you are the true
Beholder
When you look
Make sure
That you are content with
What you see
Don't mind what I say
Don't worry about the sketchy
Examples I leave
When you look
Be content with your size
Your smile
Your lines
When you look
Feel like a Queen
A King
A star
When you look
Know to love
But love yourself first
And you young men and women
Loving and acting before your time
Catch this last verse

When you look
Watch and learn
When you look
Hesitate
When you look
Try to relate
But don't let anyone
Change what you collected

And developed
Your morals
Your guides
Your history
Your inner songs
When you look
Be proud
And be strong

Did You

Did you read it w/ your parents
Did you
Did you?
Well that is why
It was called
'Soul of Mature Adolescence'
For you need them
As much as they need you
Explain it to me
Explain it to me

Replica's Mirror

I met someone
Who looked like you
Smiled like you
Had eyes like you
Told me some of the things
You use to
I knew a life with him
I couldn't live

For all must have been mere fantasy
I wanted him
To be with
Just me

Then I would live
With you
Laugh with you
Love with you
Live with you once again

| 1991 |

You Will Be The One

You will be the one
The one to betray me
Deceive me
Persuade me
To do all the things
I will never do
You will be the one
That I sit by
And say
Anything
To not have a feud
And I have been tricked
Into thinking
I've said something
To make
Someone ill willed
That's not true
I am just a mole hill
Just a liquid spill
And that is nothing
To you

You Thought

Well I had explaining to do
You thought you knew
But you never did
You were too young
And so I lived
The life trying to find
Someone like you
And look what that life
Has led me to
No you
No me
Senseless
Less sensitivity
You told me sugar and
Drinking were fine
And you were all too young
I knew then you could not be the one
Because that was which threatened me at home
Could be in your likeness
That was when you were drinking
And you hit me
And I got sick
Suburban ghetto you lived
You thought
I did you wrong
When all along
That was my song

Young Men

Young men
Too be proud of
Virginity
For if there were anything
An old man would give again
It would be the same
And the ability to not
Give it away until it is right
You can not expect
Your bride to be green
And you spotted
For you have already
Started the trail to question
What is upright

Young men
Too be proud of
Virginity
For we would all give
For it Again

Prophylactics

Let's be serious
Christians don't do it
Yet the truth is
Well
Prophylactics
Prophylactics
At least you can
Don't say you won't
Think
Life over the opposite
Test resulting what you
With it won't
Truth is some doors in the back
Remain open
Won't fit
Don't slip between the sheets
You question to know well
Truth is prophylactics
And just because they do
Don't mean you have to
Your mother told you
And if she didn't
Well
Prophylactics
Prophylactics
Prophylactics
Prophylactics
Prophylactics
AND NO DOES MEAN NO
So prevent misjudgment,
Don't even go
As perspiration and saliva
Are questionable also
Singing I don't want your kisses
And get your sweat glands to go

Seems

Seems so much of
What I say can be offensive
Just by the err of one word
Take it back
Don't say that
I don't want to look at me
Why don't you take a look at you
Do it this way
Not that
Psychobabble
Off track
No messages
Comprehensive
Misunderstood
Never Interested
I, I, I, I, I,
Yet when we hear you, you, you
We get mad
Who is we
Simply we
Who are they
Simply a mindset
Where do you want to take it
You don't know
Do we even care
It's just a show
And it seems…
So real

Standing

The Feeling Mutual

I've found a feeling mutual
I don't want to see
A mutual place
That of time
Complacent unity
Looking too deep in the perception
Which few men seam to displace?
I've found a mutual feeling
How do I say?
So rightly spaced

What

What did you say to me
Wondering if you should
Wondering if you could be
I do not know why or what it is
You anticipate
And I think you better wait

|2002|

Momma

Momma can't reach the top shelf
Lol that is funny
She may not be able to reach the sugar
But she has a lot of honey
When she has her money

Ignoring It

What is she doing
Not watching TV
Can't she understand
"That's not for me"

Never watched much
Never cared much
What makes a difference now

Watched entertainment
Within a corporation
Take Uncle Richard's Bow
Reselling it
Repackaging
Good Ruddy Luddy

What is she doing
Can't she see
It is not for me
Don't have time for it
No deficit
Just not interested
Now you see

Good Luddy Ruddy
Richard is on TV
And now they have him shaking
Baking with the oldies
Now you see
Didn't think
Any of that
Was for me

I'm watching it
Not a part of it
Nothing will change
What I feel of it
Not a darn thing
I see

Just another 40's clip
Hit 50's trip
And 60's presentation
70's with a braid unscathed
A flip of the script
A little 80's nation
MJ personification
And all is Justified
Wink Wink

Patent Me

Corporate can't patent me
If they could they would have tried
By far I am worth more than 50 an hour
401ks
Late Day and Sick
I am stronger than a brick

Small Businesses could not patent me
Doing nothing but working for nominal wage
Taking more than one position to maintain
I know to some I am not much
Though worth far more
Than a down size
And if anyone else other than myself
Could so desperately attempt
To write me up
Duplicate and sell me
Recall the day
I said I am patent free

I Didn't

I didn't expect to deal
With the Luykx of your kind
Didn't expect to creep with you
Talk to you,
Smile at you
Or even be pushed away
By the Luykx in you

Didn't seem to imagine
A person could possess
What your Luykx holds
Didn't expect a diversity
Of one scream to unfold
And it's the Luykx of your kind
I hope never to see again

| 1991 |

How

How will you allow those to break you
Lie to you
Remake you into something unlike you
Dispose of you
Ruin you
Tear you down

You won't
I won't let you
For if you allow the broken to be bond
The lie to be your truth
Become the like
Completely opposite of you
You will dispose of you
Ruin you
tear you down

I am your mother
Your father
Your sister
Your brother
Your only lover
Yourself
Your glistening water

I won't allow you to tear my strength down
When I see your fault
When I see you fail
I won't allow you to become nothing
When I see you distracted

Thinking there is a quick way
When the best way is hard work
When those that impose
Tend to tear your strength
Hear my voice
Let me rebuild you within

I am your mother
Your Father
Your sister
Your Brother
Your only lover
Yourself
All in one
Your friend

I can't allow anyone
To break the spirit God gave me
That God gave life to
I can't allow anyone
To divide the man
The woman
I made of you

As your mother
Father
Brother
Sister
Lover
Friend
You will break me
When you allow
Yourself to give in

As your mother
Father
Brother
Sister
Lover
Friend
Challenge your mind
For the alternate
Before you allow
Yourself to destruct
within

Novocain and Laughing Gas

I sat down in the chair
Took an x-ray of the maxilla region
Three needles to the inner zygomatic process
Gas to the inner membranes
Few winks of the eyes
As I saw two worlds
One with relaxation
The other I am bothered
Bothered with questions of request
World with my eyes closed
Beautiful clear day skies
As I ride adrift
I see visions of a peaceful world
Then reality asks me to rinse

| 1992 |

I Bet You Think

Bet you think I'm perfect
On purpose I left it out
And you Think I know every thing
The space within the spacing without
And you seem to see font purfectly
Misspelled in a particular place
When you think I want to be set free
They say call me on the celly
Rin g ring
I am so tired of being Molly Made
Wrong word done with intent
I am tired of being Mother N
Mother who?
What I ain't doing M right?…then
Grammar specific
Not this time
So I'll type my typos
And I hate
Hitting anyone on the hip
Well, check my zip

You Are Thinking

You are thinking I was to remain in love
When I said I love you as much as the need for blood
You are thinking I want you after all that mess
You confessed too much at mass
You could have had a bit more class
Am I still baffled
You bet your s*ss
The donkey you rode on
And the microphone you turned to stone
Through all that glass

You didn't know it
I already fell for sim
My simulated love
No apprehension
All that darn confessing you did
You should of known
You'd hurt me at last

No we never met until the time of
Case revealed
And I don't think there is a need
To love you still
So if you forgive this temperamental thing
No more thinking too fast

Blue shadows
Was it not crass?
For sure all that sitting trash
Overflowing where the food came in
Stop thinking
Perhaps it's time to pass

| 2002 |

How Can I

How can I remember the exceptional
When there is so little
How can I dispute
When I am not in contradiction
If ever you were to see
How much I can not
Surely you would understand
How I can

|2002|

A Note For You

This is a note for you
Which I know to you it won't come
It's the sorrow that I feel
For messing with our thought
Of being one
It's the day you said
I'd never get a chance again
Over and over in my head
Persistent manner
Feeling of anger
For what I did
And What we said
This is a note to you
From the new head

What they said was a gift
Was a natural tryst
A segment in a twist
An ordeal I could have missed

What they said would take time
Sped like a land mine
So deeply entwined
I would find Myself
Behind

Wicked Thin

Lucid
Lacking
Feeling unrecognized
When I didn't want to know
You insist
I take the prize

Disclosures
Alarming
Meaning displaced
No feelings to face
Words
Completely misplaced

What a wicked thin
Thing to make me see
That everything around me
Belonged to only you

Bow I see
That Wicked Thin
Thing you do
Is all so cruel
And thin wicked
You stand
With Very little
Command

Immature
Still learning
Your all over
the place
Hell is your face
Dreams you crush
With no trace

Disturbed
Confused
Your feelings
They can not show
Your sins
All a glow
Now watch the snow

What a
Wicked thin
Thing to make me see
That everything around me
Belonged to only you

Now I see
That wicked thin
Thing you do
Is all so cruel
And thin wicked \
You stand
With Very Little
Command

(To My Thirties)

My Defense

When you love me
You seem to drown me
When you are angry
I float on by
My mind tells me
That I am fine
If my defense
Takes its course in time

Then you come and
Love my love
Then I think
I'm floating above
You say not today
And I am better off
In defense gray
And I think
I need no special love
And I know
All pages unturned
Like our sheets
I remain untouched
With my defense up
And I stand here trembling
Wanting to know everything

Needing not to know you
Because if I do
If I do
My defense goes tumbling
My inner sense is fumbling
And I know not what is true
When I love you
When I think I love you

And I see me
Foolish me
Holding on to memories
Now you're gone
My defense is down
I can convince
My feelings making sense
And I know that
Things circumvent
You are coming around
My defense is down

Now I wish you to go along
Here in a sad song
You go say
I say no
My defense is up
Please shut up

No more loving
From my heart
All your self-absorbed
Talk about
Loving you all life long
We were all too right
And all so wrong

At The Well

At the well they frolic
There they play
It is a day of recognition
A day to convey
Near the flowers that bloom
A'neath a full moon
True realization
Of love in existence
Where a well runs so deep
And love for earth
Love for self
Knows no sleep

|2002|

Saving Grace

Searching for an inspiration
Thank God for a change of pace
Thank God for the time and space
It's a change of direction
A difference near perfection
And now that you have found a map
You have come hear too
Was it true?

Don't Rattle The House

Don't rattle the house
The walls may fall
Don't rattle the house
Everyone knows
That I speak in the stall
The carpet soiled
The children spoiled

Don't rattle the house
The windows may break
The cobwebs will shake
Everyone knows
I have no time for
A garden hose
Let alone fine tuning
The dust that sits on the rail

So don't rattle the house
You may want to let it be
For sanity
Wishes to remain

I Couldn't

I couldn't waste my time
Talking about something being so fine
For I've wasted my time in you
You are just an image
I am your blemish
So baby,
What do we do?

You'll call me on Monday
Talking about next Sunday
When I never see you
On either end

Yet baby,
I'm not naïve
It's plain to see
That you're living life
With your old girlfriend

So, I'm moving along
My merry way
Thinking someone will repay
For the damage you've made within
You were allowed
And it's done
No more fun
Your on run
Yes,
Though I wonder…
This is the end

|1991|

The Mind

All the time
Has pushed its way forward
Playing its little
Tricks on the mind
Just when I thought
I had all I possibly could
I am sitting near
Buying time

For it is everything
I've been
All that I have
Accomplished
What I have made
What I am to do
All of it begins
To run its time
And place
Right here with you

After Many Years...The Rat Race

After many years of working hard
She received a small banquet
And a year's free access
To the coke dispenser
How I wish I could take her space
I the one afraid
Living for the rat race
Waiting
As they sent her home
With a bouquet
And one quarter of a years entry
To a vineyard behind a closed door
Now living on a social security
Pension defaced
We are living for the rat race

Thinking Once Again

Boy you know I loved you back then
I love you now
I loved you yesterday
I love you tomorrow
As I did then

Some probably think this love
All of many
I a woman of all sorts
But it has all been for you
Our difference and cohorts
Your boys and my girls
Our love, your love, mine

You know I loved you back then
I love you now
I loved you yesterday
I love you tomorrow
Friend

All the times you talked
Of being with me
And in same breath
How my Mother was your girlfriend
You wished it to be
No matter that it hurt me

You know I loved you back then
I love you now
I loved you yesterday
I love you tomorrow
And with all sorrow
Going to take it to the top
Again
Loving you
Like your old girlfriend

|2002|

The Time I Have

The time I have is nothing less
Nothing more than spent with me
These times I appreciate are carefree
I have nothing to stand in my way
Nothing to discourage me
And I have everything
I need

|2002|

Wishing

We all have a little wishing in our hearts
We wish we had more money
Wished we'd married our first love
Perhaps an illusion of our mind
Wishing well of wells
Do tell
My true wish tonight

True
We all wish we had
A chance to travel
To all Four Corners of the world
Though round
We
Love the art of wishing

Wishing to move
To the brighter side of life
Wishing well
Do Tell
What it is I strive

Bliss

Thinking every moment
Loving him
Feeling
Bliss
Knowing his every word
His every breath
He is bliss

Wanting his every frontal
Lateral turn to be
All my own
Needing him
Wanting him
Yearning
Bliss

Entwined in a kiss
For he is the Bliss
Of my morning
Like a cup of coffee
He is the bliss
Of my evening
A pecan pie cooled over
He is the king of my life
Closer than alpha and omega
Can be to God
He is my bliss
For him
My love
Will forever be
Assigned

Semblance of Insanity

Sometimes I become so flustered
I choose not to write
Any man could understand
If he could explain all of life's mysteries

Sometimes I even see the papel pintado amarillo
Closing in on me
I can't breathe
I see the darkness
I cry
Becoming cold
Stock brokers on wall street would explain it
If only they could justify an economic slow downs

At times I get the notion to walk back in time
Sit with Eliot or Pound in an asylum
And watch life fly by
Through my mind
I even wish to reconstruct past time
To make things perfect
To reassemble reason

There is just some semblance of insanity
That my mind cries to
That all men do

Sometimes I wish I could make means justifiable
Right and wrong
The tree of life would describe it to you
If it could speak

Sometimes I wish I could compromise without negotiating
Without having to put on a mask
When I really don't like things

My ancestors
Would describe it to you
If they could tell it from the grave

There is just some semblance of insanity
That my mind cries to
That all men do
And the earth still revolves

If I Could

If I could kiss your lips
Stroke your ear
Hold you and everything
You say dear
If I could
I think I would take you
Somewhere else

If I could tell you
You have always been admired
Set your heart on fire
And you know I question
Tights
But If I could
I would
And there would be nothing but us

And I know you wouldn't mind
I know you would say
Cherish and honor
I give you this day
I know you would understand me
I know you would not harm me
I believe I could trust you
Even though I truly know
I can't

Was That You

It took so much of me to figure out
If that was you

You should have been concerned
You knew the truth
Times held gaps
Appearances were lack
So I had to ask
Was that you?

Faced with decisions
Every chance I gain
I manifest to you
That you are alone with me
And I still had to ask
Of you
Was that you?

And do you care
How I may be smashed
How the gametes of my life
Will no longer produce
And years from now
For something
I should have known
I will ask
Was that you
In pain
Was that you

Yet pain is something
Of the mind
Told by you to me to endure
For it makes me stronger
And from all the things

I've learned from you
I've asked
Was that you?

That within me cries out
To you and says "You too Taker"
"Taker, are you sure that is you?"
My dear,
Is that you?

| 1991 |

And There

And there it is again
The symbol of affection
The rose
Hawthorne thought of it
Waller used it
Many took pride in it
And I bring it to you to say
It is not a symbol just yet
Of affection
Though a pain too
The thorns piercing
The hurt came through
The blood rushed from my hand
To be the strength the rose
Longed for growth
Pushing forth red petals
Showing others its symbol of society
I'd be damned if I didn't get
Credit was stolen
As it took from me

It's the same rose
Sitting in the corner
As it shriveled
That is worthless rose
Lost control
And died
No more to show affection
But the process of life
We all go through

| 1991 |

I Have

I have lived and died through you
For I have laughed with a sobriety
Which lead me to be insane
I loved again
And fear
For love is something to be afraid of
As the tears flow from my womb
My heart
My eyes
Eyes to the heart
Womb to ground

That which was within
Like love
Has conceived
Grew
Then died
Force of death

Right now
We have died
I have cried
A tear too many
Yet future may hold for
Conception of love
And that which was
Within
Once more

| 1991 |

Somewhere In Time

Do you hear me?
I said I love you
I am sure this is something
I can do

Do you hear me
I said I need you
I knew that
The day I laid eyes on you

I see you waiver
You seem to threaten
Well that can be a little cute
But as they say
It must be fate
For the first time
I can relate

If you hear me
I said I love you
And now I am saying yes
Now inviting you
To take over
Please don't take
My last breath
We are somewhere in time

I Had

I had to build things
To what it should have been
You berate us
We love you
You slap us
We make you whole
And you keep on slapping
And we stand for it all
Perhaps I had to renew myself
With hopes of bringing all
The sisters along with me
We are more than a turn
Here or there
We are more than a one night
You turned to a flagrant affair
How could you expect nothing but
When you call them in your ruts
In the same pant calling for The Queens
Atrocious affairs deserve anything but

I Know

I know that you are there
Somewhere
Far but so close to be near
And I thought I'd let you know
I am close to letting go
That I don't believe
In what it is that transpired
And now my heart is turning fire
For something I don't see
Something I don't trust
Something I know not
Something I fear to love
And the words of the streets
Come in to invade
Telling me it's no good
I am walking into sin
That you are not real
And love will never be the same
And I will never love again
For too much has corrupt my brain
And I want to but I can't
And I want to but I won't
And I want to but I can't see
And because of that I sit back
and believe this is fantasy
and realize I live in a different
actuality
So perhaps it is time
To put me back
Because I no longer believe
In the world so far off track

My Quilt

Going To Church

Going to church
And coveting what I am in
Going to church
And coveting what a sin
Coveting cars
Coveting homes
Coveting wealth
And still
Going to church and coveting
Birth rights give by God

If You Know

That's if you knew
I have a history
You would turn to page thirteen
Trickle, trickle, trickle
One said paragraph four
To me
That's if you knew of Katz
And heritage hidden
You would know of Langston
And Rickett
And speak of words unspoken on leaflet fifteen
Where injuries of me behold
Word obscurity

Some say no unity
Some say right as wrong as he
Skipping to twenty nine
And circa 1653
Indi-Afri
Afri Afri
Leaflet thirty six is the story
The mix red black black red
Truly eyes will see
I'm free
I'm free
Always have so truth will be

So I walked with a cane that day
Backwards through the door
The pain in my leg excruciating
It was beyond soar
Talked about the weather
Admin said it wasn't clever
So she social to my door
And took the life out of mine and self

And I'm thinking defamation
The way she continues to harass is plain
See when I left and said that Princeton would be no more
I returned to hell I came
Returned to hell I came
And she sits like she is not to blame

Mother Orange Glo'

If they only knew
Of Mother Orange Glo'
Her strength
In time of need
The drive
For her children to succeed
Is more than
A soccer mom's commute
Mini-van of children
PTA dash
Or baking pan
Mother Orange Glo'
Spells Dreams in sand
And pillars of land
The common men crave
Going to support efforts
For a struggle in the Mother Land
Mother Orange Glo'
Has tennis in her hand
And enduring man
Strength of many
In a smile
Her female seeds
Bring green from the Nile

Where We Hail

Urban Jersey Homage

It's where we hail
from the pits to the nut
It's where we hail
Like a bleeding open cut

We take the juices
We become affluent
To only prosper in creativity
What do you expect?

We come from the tri area
Where we are surrounded
By art, music and style
It seeps in the air

For there is nothing
That compares
To what we make
What they take

For heaven's sake
No child should know
What we know
But it is
What we see

It's known we are rich
With this
So our
Neighborhoods
Are said to be tainted
We won't know
We believe

But we soar like angels
We breathe all angels
Henceforth no excuse
It is not accepted
When we say we can not
Achieve

We Never

We never needed
To scream and holler
To get our point across
Brother I said I heard you
Sister I said
Your words
Come clearly
From your mouth
No need to shout
all seemingly reminiscent
From what we learned
At home
We seem to stop
And Scream
At the zone
When it's done
All I hear is
A tangled jargon
From whose mouth?

But you say
You speak in tongues
And no
I don't scream
See we seem
To transfer
This form of communication
Back to our youth
This aggressive dispute
For a hidden agenda
We exhale the breath
Of a guide
And they seem to hover
To our side

The words tend
To make sense
All of relativity
But some of us
Are saying that
Aggression is not me
Repetitively
Repetitively
Repetitively
For we don't want the cycle
Of the angry
Living all through our veins
All through our wombs
All through our homes
And surely not
At the place of green paper
Re: the point
We never need
To holler or scream
To relay

He Said

He said I want to teach you
To be a man
He said to his little boy
So he would understand

I have no plans to
Ever leave your side
He said
As he looked
His little boy
In his beautiful
Brown eyes

I have every intention
Of doing what is right
He said as he cleaned
His wife's ring
As the little boy said
It shines

I want you to see a man
That stays in your life
Takes care of his wife
His family
I want you to learn from me

He said I want you to
Learn to work and save
Invest
We don't need name brand
Sometimes generic
Says it best

Seep Into Me

Seep Into Me

Seep into me
Or let me seep into you

Let me absorb your every breath
As if I were you

Let me experience the extremity
Of your personal being
As I hope you too
Want from me

Let me learn to love again
Through you
By you
And with you

If I were to think
Of many of a lonely days
I lived
I would be moved
Only to rejoice
That I have renewed and begun
With you

So I am left to say
Seep into me
Or let me say
Allow me to seep into you

Let me absorb
Your every micro-being
That makes your macro being
Complete

Let me live through you my dear

|1991|

Ramsey

This it to my Ramsey
You know what I mean
I'm back to machine
Were you suppose to get me something
Scam
Ripped to the seams
I'm not in your dreams
And when you didn't want me anymore
I had more shoes
I knew who was not due

I Think I am Afraid

Will I love you too much
Will I need you too much

Will I suffocate you
Will we love like
We are suppose to

Baby if I don't love you
Right
Please forgive my
Oversight
Of the beautiful being
You are

How I wish to nurture you
I want to love you
Till I don't understand
I want to kiss you
Until all my wishes come true
I want to caress you
Until you confess
That you are blue
When I am not with you

|2002|

I Just Knew

I just knew that I could never live
That feeling again
Then you arrived
And showed me differently

You showed me
I could laugh again
Within Sanity
Love again
And not fear
Yet you haven't showed me
The tear that damns love
To a termination

Oh how God composed love
To be conceived,
Mature,
And die
I hope we would only mature
And unite into infinity
Yet infinity expands to forever
And love is not just enough
To stand for that time

So, I could only sit and watch you
And you watch me
And the controller of love
Watch us
To decide if we should mature
Should we die
Then to conceive
All over again
Or shall we see
The love tear of termination

Nothing To Act as an Accompanist Anymore

I walked in the kitchen
To feed my stomach
Decided I wanted a potato
Realized I,
That sour cream was not there
Nothing to act as an accompanist anymore

Out the front door
I went to roam the streets
I felt compelled by some insignificant touch
To do so
Realized I
That the streets were all that were there
No sidewalks to e found
Nothing to act as an accompanist anymore

Into my mind,
I flee
A vision of I and he
Though in my life
He no longer exists
Nor did the deceit
Nothing to act as an accompanist anymore

From the stomach
To the dendrites
From the dendrites
To my mind
Am I living a hell
When there is
Nothing to act as an accompanist anymore

I went next door to visit Mrs. Michell
She was no longer Mrs. But Miss Dishevel
Her husband left her with an unfair settlement
She has two children
No longer a housewife
I do believe
Nothing to act as an accompanist anymore

I went to the church
Where the Deacon was the Preacher
The place I were to marry you
Yet realized I,
That would never come true,
Nothing to act as an accompanist anymore

I slept by your side
I slowly awaked
I showed you all
You never had to anticipate
You and she were speaking of your past
Then of your future
Realized I,
That you were making a mistake
You too would see
That there was
Nothing to act as an accompanist anymore

From divorce
To marriage
To a mistake
Am I living a hell
When there is,
Nothing to act as an accompanist anymore

I looked for that melody
The one
I know he speaks to me
No longer he spoke
For he was not in harmony

And there was
Nothing to act as an accompanist anymore

Into my heart
I slid
With an ice pick to rid
What was nearly of stone
His love
Cut me to the bone
Though no more
And never the less I say,
Nothing to act as an accompanist anymore

I saw his face
Felt nothing could replace
The kindness
The warmth
He brought everyday
Yet with that face as an exterior
I had not to see the interior
And I was blind
In this I say
Nothing to act as an accompanist anymore

From my ears
To my heart
From my heart
To my eyes
Am I living a hell
When there is
Nothing to act as an accompanist anymore
|1991|

You gave too much time
For the dressing
Over cooked bird
With distressing
Left my love abandoned
And it's not anew

Three years of undressing
Two months of your messing
Five minutes on the remodeled floor
Six months of baby-sitting blues
Guess? (Bull h sit)
Go find someone else to use

Shall Be We

When I feel that you can understand me
And one day you will
You will see that it is
You will know what you see
You will understand all that is
And all that is
Shall be we

When you love me as I adore you
When I adore you as I love you
As no man or woman stands before you
You will know my love is real
Like Baldwin to the tusks
Like the ring that shines so much
I want to know the Lord...
And I know I have found him

And if any man can hold a torch
To the flame that burns in me
It could only be the man
That has set my soul freeeee
And now you are all in me
He has swept me off my feet

For All The Seeping

Always saying
Seep into me
Or that is let me
Seep into you
When I was
Truly wishing
You would flip over
That accrued

Seep to this
Seep to the one you miss
Seep to the replica
You tried to make
Tell her you were creeping
On Sunday

Seep to this
Ask her to kiss the kiss
I laid down on Saturday
Seep to this
And may your bliss be damned

Seep to the Fridays you picked
Me up
Was she out of town?
Seep to this
Thursdays I wished hell
To be your ground
Now you are wishing for the wrong
Liquid to seep
Because the viscosity
Is far too complex
For your seeping to be

On Wednesday
When I sent your mail
You should be glad
Your pancakes weren't stale
Hear me on Tuesday when
I leave her the note
That on Monday you won't
Be seeping with me again
I heard it is her friend

Now seek to weep for this
Last line
And tell your mother
You messed up this time
With your tainted gray sheets
And all that seeping
Blotted your foolish mind

Round - A - Bout

You send me on a Round a bout
Round-a-bout your life, I am
I am the Round a bout of present
Most likely the Round-a-bout of future

You release the latch of bodily gravitational suspension
Leaving me pinned against the wall
With neither ground or sky to support me
To hold me

Constantly I am oblivious
Maybe you will come to rescue me
Though we know that's a lie
Therefore, there's no future for us
No sensible one anyway

Our lives go about and around
In circles
You're the dog
Chasing the cat
With a harsh barking
A yell
In a round-a-bout way
Don't bite your own tail

You are the jackal
That laughs at the innocent she-ass
Who gave the new experience
Who hurled
In a round-a-bout way

You send me
In turn
I'll send you
In a round-a-bout

| 1991 |

He said
This is how
You get back at me
No
I write despair
If anything
I write that feelings now
Could never be shared

Love Don't Know Love

Love doesn't know love
The way this love
Wants to know you
Sky doesn't know blue
And Seagulls know of no sea

Love doesn't live wide
And breathe freely
Love holds friends
At arms length
Because
Love doesn't know me

Like love knows self
And if anyone else knew love
They would say her guard fell
If love knew love
They way love knew you
They'd know
The meaning of detrimental

It Has Come

For it has come
And I can't see it
For there to be mere
That seems so distant
Hence since the last breath
You have breathed was the scorpions touch
Seems your broth has toiled
With something so untrue
Your words
Your whispers seem so faint
Here me I can't cry anymore
We all know that the art of bacteri
in our skin and knives to cut the stress
of years can not truly hide the pains
we both have
And neither of us will come
Herein are you listening hearing but not
consuming
For I can truly say your pains
Are in need of a peace
And my eyes are in need of same
You want me to turn on you
Said business is not like that
I don't understand the games of this
And I don't care to fight back
There is always someone misinterpreting
Everything
And everything is not always about everyone
Per chance you prefer I lie to you
What good would I ever be for you
And if and when that day comes
A bridge should be crossed for unity
I pray it does not collapse
Because of all that has been done to we

The keenest eyes do not understand
That love will love for love only
For if there was a comprehension
They would not have asked
Love loves for the soul
Love loves for the brain
Love loves for the heart
And as brethern and friend love loveth you
But love can't lie to you
Love must be straight forward
Or love can be no more

Soon they'll know
What couldn't show
When it touched the snow
It couldn't grow
Soon they'll know
What called it beau
Now calls it foe

Can't You See

Can't you see that hides
Behind these eyes
Do you hear the heart that calls
do you see the eyes water
To the thought of you
Have you connect the puzzle
To realize the distance
Is from the need of your touch
To extend
And help what is hurting within

What we lack is communication
An interactive gap exists
A conversation
I will strike
So that you will speak
And I will learn
And I will speak
And you will learn
And the fear
Will no longer be there
It will flow from my eyes
In a river of tears

What we lack is trust,
What we have proclaims to be
Something that will not be
Beneficial to a relationship
That could hold
And you will sit in front of me
and speak
I will hear
Hopefully one day
You will too

You will hear a heart
That calls to you
It's message being
Trust is what
It needs from you
If only you would speak
Then the fear
Would run
From eyes aqueous

What we have is a hindrance
A detour in our desires
To want to be with one another
We, afraid
Though if I could wipe
Past slate clear
Then you can too
And you would
To see eyes that water abundantly in joy

And you will know when my heart
Makes a call for you
That which will manifest to you
A part of it that it needs
And the tears which became streams
Will no longer flow
My need for touch
Will by then have become yours
We will have understood
And the need will become no more
For it will be fulfilled
But are you taking heed?

I Said

I said I love you
The first time
I looked at you
I said I love you
The first time
I saw your smile
All in one day
All in one way
I knew you
Would make my life
Worthwhile
I said I love you
When you looked
My way
And how I longed
To wait for the day
That I would kiss your lips
Stare into your eyes
And say
Never say good-bye
For I love you forever
And a lifetime

Did I Love You

When my eyes set
Upon you unglued
I never knew what I did

We unmet
You would not let
Me into you
What I did I never knew

Until you were ready
Your conscious mind
You're the Zeus
I am yours waiting
What was known I never did

Through your turns
Your holds
Your pause
Your launch
What I was the known never did

In comparative
The first thrown out
When they found
Touches were a sin
Became ungodly
To knowledge of truth
The known never did what I was

For when I was thrown
From Godly grace
You reversed my mistake
And I became untouched
With knowledge of truth
I then knew what I did
I loved you

Society II

To The Soldiers

I just wanted to tell you
Though I do not know you
That you are my hero
And far more than I could ever be
I just have to tell you
That if I could look into your eyes
I would be a coward
For you would see a sister
Fearing for you
Grateful for you
Praying for you
Taking your breaths with you
Thanking you
Crying with you
Smiling with you
I am praying for you
Living your pain
Knowing you will be fine
If you only remember
That the Strong Prevail
Prevailing without fear
Whether not in our decision
We know in our hearts
The strong Prevail
Prevailing without fear
And I thank you from my soul
And I want you to recall
When you recall
Prevail without fear
Recall
Me being grateful for you
Me praying for you
Me taking breathes with you
Me thanking you

Me crying with you
Me smiling with you
Me praying with you
Me living your pain
Then perhaps you will remember
For fear you need not
Your living is never in vain

In Life's Fright

She had a boyfriend in her town
One in the borough
Who would have known?
Her sorrow felt
When a complex unfurls

He had a girlfriend in
The Dorm
One in the North Too
Seemed to favor company
With those of the far West show
Who would have known
His sorrow when
Things turned
Worse than chlamidic

They had a marriage so strong
They thought as one crept
To the night of horror
Embarking on Aids of delight
The other at home
With a boyfriend of she
Who knew a girlfriend of he
All entwined
In life's fright

Recession Confession

This is a true recession confession
And when it come to feed
Know your need
When it comes to clocked time
Double trip and rewind
When time clues deed
We will not recede

The Five Minute Documentation
Of The Older Woman's Cry

I wish I were thin
I wish I were young again
I wish I didn't have to do
The domestic things I do
Wishing not to have stretch marks
Not to be awakened in the middle of the night

I wish you were obese
You were old
You were working until you dropped
Wishing gravity would pull you
Deplete you
And take your breast and butt to the ground

I wish you were ugly
Wishing you not to be flirtatious
To only say
It's you I wish to be

| 1991 |

Rogue Child

Rogue child
Illicit
Tell your mother to take
Off that she things she wed with
That the one she wed is not
The same
As your father
Who's name do you bare

So if female
Is it hard for you?
To grow up hating men
In their absence
Will you not trust
In fear that will vanish

Is it just for you
If male
To turn to another
On the streets
Saying the Older ones
Will love and guide me

Everyone
Come and see
Look at the Rogue Child
Watch it now
And stay for a while
See the difference between it
And a sanctioned

How soon we forget
That the status of the parents
Should not determine
How the child is treated
That of division
Which with ignorance and disgust
We can look at the rogue child
How ugly we are

| 1991 |

The Old Lady

You want to talk about snowy days
How hard it was for her to find
A job to bring home pay
That old Lady
That Old Lady
Some in this place think nothing of

I say you want to take from an old lady
An old lady that had nothing from slavery
Nothing from her family's sharecropping days
Hear me now as I speak from the grave and the living

You want to take to make more money for you
Sins of your sins
Your father is coming through
Some say what do we care
We've what we want
And you ask me why I am so angry
And I took a look at you

The old lady gave me gravy when you didn't
Think to look my way
Now you want to take her pension and
Deliver me to be insane
But I am living for the old lady
And going to break it down this way
I am living for the old ladies
Going straight into judgment day
When I am an old lady haunting
Those in likeness of those judged
In their sleep

They won't sleep
They won't sleep
Hush now don't you peep
Feeding of her breast
While beating her father's back
The strength of the old lady is coming here
And hitting you back
For the old lady sips her gravy
And the old lady is now me
I won't allow you to do this
And I won't allow you to feed off of me

Every Woman

(For Epiphany)

And every woman should be equipped
With a lever burned
Or a remote control
In hand
For the gift you given
For the pain driven
In return she could give
To a man she think to love
With the idea that he will
Know commitment
Then in turn she will burn
Then in turn she will say
You should have known
You could not play
She was not
Yesterday's video game
Game Over
Now
Who's sorry

My Cry of Understanding

God put me through a hell
So I can cry tears of many
God put me through this hell
So I can see the shades plenty
God knows the waters get deep
So he holds me so strong
God put me through this hell
So I know that all
Is capable of going wrong
And I am silent
So silent
Because the hell I know nothing of
As God holds me so strong
So he may teach me to sing his song
And I sing so loud
And no one listens
And I sing so proud
And my tears glisten

God wants me to know life
So that I am aware of death
God knows all strength in me
That is why he has put me in
This test
Don't worry if I seem so far away
If you are real
My heart will forever stay
Until then
Let God work in me
And turn his spirit free
Let God do his work
So when I speak
I'm understood
I'm interested

I'm freedom
But the freedom seems insane
I'm interested in freedom
But the pictures live in vain
This is my understanding
This is my cry of comprehension

Stay…And stay strong with God

They Say They Want Songs

They say they want songs
Songs of what ?
Agony
They say Iraqi Freedom
How many are they say
Singing this wanting this
While we sing
Freedom Ring
Seven alarms of warning
Rung
Bombing over Baghdad
What Song
Singing they don't know
The domino affect
They don't know
The calls we may reap
All for the songs that
They want sung
But here on edge
We now live
Not wanting to get
On a plane for a bit
Here we breathe
Ever so lightly
Some not thinking that
It was the soot filling the lungs
Where they stood
While we sing
Freedom Ring
It is a song unsung
For the laborers are many
And the war is not one
When our decision is solo
And our need will always be

For a song we all sing
Internationally

This is for the songs
They want sung
When we should have been singing
Peace a little louder
Should have been singing United
United United
Sure enough it was Divided the bombs fell
United we never were
Divided this nation prevailed
Prevailed for those not eating
Prevailing for those not able to do
Anything but remain glued to the TV
In presence of fear
Do they hear
Do they hear
A nation surviving on fear
No longer flying
No longer buying
Just scared

I Want You

I want you to understand
That I haven't been the perfect sister
Haven't been good to you at all
Through the years

My soul wants to be with you
On that battle field
My soul wants to be near you
Being your shield

I want you to understand
That I was selfish and ignorant
While you were on base
I stayed in School just three miles from you
Never visiting

And now my soul wants to cry for you
My brother is in the air
My soul wants to be near you
Being your shield

I want you to know that I am scared
For what you are doing
What you were not
Trained to be
You are an loving individual
Always setting my heart free
I am the one that cries
I am the one that will worry

For if there is one thing that harms you
I will never live the same again
As I cry this very moment
I am angered deep within
For the decision makers
Wanted this war
For whose own they should have sent
For if I loose you now
My life will be lost again

Embarrassment of Greed

For your fine luxury cars
For your travel expenses
For your motor homes
And gas that should not be their fuel
For your sweet broken memories
Of what it was to be poor
You said you never knew it
You said never more
So for them you think
You would go and show them even more
We feel so good about ourselves
Sitting in the local pubs
Drinking and Drinking
And not thinking
Have we all forgotten
That which was the best for us all
Did we not learn about ethics
Did we not learn about diversity
Did we not learn about kindness
Or was it in the Sunday pew
We sat questionably
Praying to Jesus
And smirking at our friends
I want your rich gold
I'll only take ten
With or without it being sold
I say there are other alternatives
What if there was a need no more
This is for my embarrassment of greed
Greed money and green
This is for my embarrassment of ignorance
All this land of opportunity
Based on intelligence
And at times we seem so senseless
Loving concepts

Alone

Alone a man walked along
Speaking to all of his own
That of himself
Not in misery

Another stood and watched
For the man once known
Walked and talked
Aloud alone

And many now call him crazy
To I,
I figure it a bit hazy

For that man who spoke to something
We could not see
Knew something
Which we could not believe
Which he knew was sanity

Sanity which was a friend
A friend to comprehend

| 1991 |

Love Of A Country

This is for the love of a country
And the pride I seldom show
Just thought I would let you know
This is for the love of a country
Standing at the doors of war
Nothing considered left or right
When knocking on someone's floor
The love of a country for I stay neutral
The love of a country for I am the pupil
Loving a country
See how it loves me back
Think
Think
Think about that
As I sit loving a country
My thoughts on track

Raspberry Sorbet

And I bathed my body in raspberry sorbet
I feeling good about the heat I receive
I feeling pain run from my body
I feel a fool to bathe the stains away
The stains of your blood
The stains of my blood
The stains of the soil
How dirty I feel today
The stains of my heart
Never taught to fight
The pains of my soul
Tormented so
I bathed my body in raspberry sorbet
Knowing truthfully the pain of war
Will never go away
And how ugly my bath looks now
Filled with raspberry stains
Raspberry pains
The water will never be clear
It is all in my brain

The Truth Of It

Everything is Temporary

The day I was born
Was a temporary thing
Every Monday of January
Which hits the fourteenth day
Can not hit back to seventy-two

The life of a dog or any animal
As well as a human
Is living something on a notion
On some timely basis
To conclude in ones mind
That living is temporary

One friendship to the other
I go
She was no good
He was no better
I moved from North to South
They no longer had a place
In my life
Temporary friendships
Are beyond my head

I live in Willingboro
In Trenton,
Plainsboro, East Orange,
Ewing and Greensboro too
All in the same year
Just to prove to myself
That my home is my body
And my body at times
Has no home
For the simple fact
That our living
Situations are temporary

A child have I
A baby
Ten months ago
A cell
Ten years from now
An adult
To go on
Leave me
And marry
To have children
Of own
Everything is
Temporary
Even death is
A temporary Thing

You Don't

You don't appreciate me
You don't understand me
You don't listen to me
You don't hear me
You kno---w
How I---
When w---e
Do that
You see
How I ---
Feel when

Can you hear me
You don't love me
You don't see me
You walk right through me
You chastise me
You don'----t
Hear me
You don't
We don't

How are you going to say that
You won't
You won't watch my back
You wil----l
I wil---l
We wil---l
Do that wrong again

You don't know me
You don't think of me
You won't give me
I won't render you
We won'---t

You don'---t
We can'----t
Try again
We tried
It died
You see
A love end
Cause you don't
You don't
I don't
We won't
You don't
I don't
We won't
Again

Your Face

Children
You are the heroes and heroines
Yes the soldiers that have gone off
Those that will return are same
But I call your names
You are the heroes and heroines
Children
You put up with our decisions
You give us the strength to thrive
You are the heroes and heroines
Children and I thank you for
Taking us grown ups for the ride

I'm Not Perfect

I'm not perfect
At night I wear fluffy shoes
During the day
I decide if I will brush my hair
Or let it remain to be in disarray
I am not perfect
Some times I yell
When I should whisper
Some times I pray all day
At times I work for play
And if you think I am not perfect
Then you know you agree too
For I am not perfect
And I wonder are you not perfect
Too
For if so
Perfection is something
Neither of us should worry
For imperfection is just fine
I'm not perfect
And for which no one is paying me
A dime

Something I Can't Have

It's when you are gone
I want you back
Your nose
Your lips
Your eye contact
I'm so in need of you
Your stance
Everything you do
I refuse to let you slip away
Your kisses have me trembling
Your whispers
Baby oh so real
Truly I adore you
But I'm in love
With something new
Something I can not have
In love with someone
I can not see
And for him I can not be
Your touch
Your feel
I can't resist your face
Your voice
I want you right here
But I am so scared
And I run
Though I said yes
My mind says no
And I'm in love
With something new
Something I can not have
Truly one I can not see
And for him want to be
But this was all in my head

From ten to one
He's counting and
It's all over again
In love with who
Someone new
Someone I can not have
When will your
Heart be for me

Selfish Poetry

This is to you
I write
With selfish poetry
All of my life
Is me
All about I
Till I die
My selfish poetry

I only write
What I know
I knew you
I wrote
And as is
It's selfish poetry

Life I lived
Was there
No one knew
I cared
About anything
That is everything
And it's
Selfish poetry

Feelings within
They stood
And all they knew
Was that I did write
What I would
And that in completion
Is selfish poetry
To understand me
Is to love what is selfish
Selfish poetry

My
I
Till I die
Redundantly
I reveal selfish poetry

Reciprocal Tip

The Documentation of
The Older Woman's Cry

I wish I were thin
Young
I wish I didn't have to do
The domestic things I do
To wish not to have stretch marks
Not to be awakened in the middle of the night
For anyone's appetite

I wish you were obese
Old
You were working
Until you dropped
I wish gravity
Would pull you
Dispense you
And take your breast and butt
To the ground

I wish you were not as pretty
To wish you to not be flirtatious
To only say to you
I wish
I were you

| 1991 |

Dear Daddy

I heard the tune
The flute
The bassoon
I think to thank you now
For what you've given me
The house
Was fine
The food
On time
You worked so hard
Now I see
I want to thank you now
For that given me

You were
Always on the road
At times in the cold
From West to East
You gave musical feast
Yes, I seemed to have miss
Bits of the grits
You prepared for me
When the mic was in your hand
And you were raising
Your hands
I want to thank you now
For what you gave me
Yesterday, Today, Tomorrow
I have all intentions to repay

You must be mistaken
You thought you knew God
Turned around
And thought you had a feeling profound
Walking and talking
With wings you called prayer...
Looked around and saw that Judas was near

Funny how he held you close
And rubbed your elbows
Stroked your toes
And crowned you with emperor's clothes
Words in command
You hold and calling for an exit
Will I hold my tongue?
It's burning for reflex
I guess I'll stay poor
Because when I feel like complaining
I'll do it

Someone forgot what they were doing
But realized the devil put them to it
Claiming Jesus using the daily news
For the fame
Where will you put your time?
As in mine you need not stain

In me you will only find God
It's a shame that you have it all wrong
For the devil came and robbed it all
 He took your soul
Your mind and made you whole_

Will I worry if the boat is missed
Because the pole that dropped held the blood with Judas
.... Got to watch it move on got to keep my pure heart pure
Even if the devil follows
He will know my score

For he's walking around
Everything he borrowed
To rid children of hope
Their dreams for tomorrow

And if you see him let him know
That God is really sound
Though he think when his eyes
Close on this earth
All beyond is not true
He said you might want to know
God is coming for you

And as in many stories told
Will you know what form he will hold
All the children whose dreams
You left untold
The earth's crust has split for you
Perhaps now it will fold

She Said

She said I am not interested
Take it all back
Whatever you are selling
I will stay broke
And on Track
So if you think you have love
It is ice instead
Now please consider that

She said I don't know
What you think I've got
But what it is
You won't want anymore
She heard his dialect
Closed the door to the unsaid
So if you think you have love
It is ice instead
Consider that

She said I am not turning him over
I am not turning it out
I will not give my children
I don't care what it is about
You don't want this
I'll turn
And all too familiar scene
Be-love me
So if you think you have love
It is ice instead
Get off my back

He Said

All I want to do is love you
All I want to do is know you
All I want to do is provide for you
All I want to do is be beside you
So if love don't want me
I'll bring the heat
If you think you are through with this
Be prepared for the hot seat

He said
All I want to do is kiss you
All I want to do is make you feel good
All I want to do is write with you
All I want to do is sing your songs
So if love don't want me
I'll bring the heat
If you think you are done
Meet defeat

People Will

They will talk to you
They will talk about you
They will open their mouth
And criticize all the things you do
They will call you stupid
They will call you dumb
But you are so much more than that
You are what they abhor
You are a strong woman
You are a wonderful man
You are a beautiful child
Building castles in many sands
You are heritage
You are history
And people will
Dine on you
And attempt to kill
But your strength is you
Your essence true
Your beauty so deep
You are health
Not weak

Long Flowing Hair

She had long flowing hair
Around Page four or six
But it was the only way
She was to get many
In the mix
The had a pure loving heart
With no premonition
That she was caught up
In a bunch of tricks
Good for her she knew of her
Identity
With her long flowing hair
She knew truthfully
The end result
Was to be told
They say what was sold
Was the confusion of
Long flowing hair
And translucent eyes

Engulfed

Engulfed
Hanging on
Every word you say
And loving you afar
Engulfed
Your neck, your arm
Your face, your
Embrace is what I want
Loving you here
Thinking Thinking
Of What it will take
To get there by your side
There in your mind
There in your life
This is crazy
And that love has been
Done before by you
This is crazy
I thinking I am another number
For you
And quickly you will drop me
Drop me
Leaving me once again to love
Alone

Reciprocal Tip

Is my life so perfect
That I become so quick
To judge another

Let man believe in the superficial
Supernatural
Superhuman
Things he does
And let I not sit
And look
And say
That his life
Is not lived
The correct way
The reciprocal tip
Will carry weight
The reciprocal tip
Will come to repay

If only I sat to think
If every man
Were to act like me
What a non-God
Needing, Believing
World
This would be

| 1991 |

Never is Now

Never experiencing such I have now
There is always something breaking me down
Pulling me from knowing you
Loving you afar
Won't do
And since I can't have you now
For more than a friend
Let me get close to you
And love you till the end
The end of all times
The end of all whispers
The end of all my nightmares where you don't exist
I said let me be your sister baby
So I can grow to be your friend
And after my decisions have been made
I'll close all the wounds of the heart
That need to mend
Saying let me be your friend

Now No Longer Never

Now wanting you near
Knowing this will be soon
Can't stand having you so far away
Want your love for me to manifest soon
Knowing that you are becoming weak
As your last breath you are holding on to
I have to have you near
As our love in limbo holds nothing true
And since I can't have you now
I will wait until then
For I am wanting you more and more
More than your brother
More than your friend
I am willing to take it all on
Pull you out of your hell
Reconstruct with you
Singing let me be your brother sister
Let me be your mentor mister
Let me be your lover brother
And all the more for you
Yet you must understand
Until the day comes
I will silently wait for you
It was what we were born to do
I was born dedicated to you

Trying Times Mommy

These are trying times for me Mommy
I am in need of your love and guidance
If you could spend the night and remove the fright
There would be nothing that can go wrong
But we all sing this song
Song of war

These are trying times for my Mommy
If you could hold me close
Love me still
Make my mind and body agile
Soothe my soul
Keep me whole
For I feel a bit confused
For you told me to love
You told me about the world
You told me about the triune
And these are trying times for me Mommy
We all seem to be getting ill
I pray
One day the trying times
Will stand still

Clarity

You Want Your Papers

You think I will love you
When you know nothing of
Loving me
Come and get your papers
Let's set this soul free

You want to berate me
Mar my spirit
Kill my entity
Deflate my sensibility
Come and get your papers
Set your soul free

You don't know me
You don't love me
You don't kiss me
You won't miss me
Come get your papers
You know we need to be free

Papers to release me
Papers to exclude me
Papers to financially
Oh yes, include me
Papers to null and void us

Come and get your papers
Cause I can not
Stay still
And be here
With you

…but wait
I hear the voices that say
I should stay
I hear the children laugh
And play
I hear them sad when
Our words are stray
Hide the papers
Maybe we can work it out
Hide the papers
I don't want sad mouths
Hearts
Minds
And Frowns
And did I think
What living single again
Would be
In a world of confusion
And HIV
Exclude the signatures
Roll them up
And place them
Afire
Let's stick this out
In our irony
And mire

He Wants Clarity

He wants clarity
She said incognito
"Ambrosial"
He wants
Some clarity
She said
"sshshshshhow enough"
He said he wants some clarity
She said
"The Door"
Cause brother lover
There ain't much more
Till you have her
Completely floored

Purple Velvet

Moving around in her purple velvet
You must be mistaken
For the color
Is meant in symbolism
You better read your literature
For realism
Moving around in purple velvet
Because the words so harsh
The fabric had to mend
Oh purple velvet soothing like satin
Purple velvet all in Walker's Head
Sugar you hear me screaming
When MY Mister says its dead
Moving around in purple velvet
For freedom
She wrote Hemorrhage in My Head

You Must Have

You must have mistaken me
For someone who gave a damn
About what you were thinking
Thinking Then
Thinking When
You thought you were Cassius
And I retorted as Frazier
And you must have
For the times you said
You can not prove the abuse
Executed on the mental state
And I gave you an upper punch
Coming out with a TKO
In the last round
You found your ground
You thought my name was Scarlet
How far you were dear Sir
Oh how Russ thought he whispered
As Andrea softly purred
As said before
Wind Here Done Gone
Yes, You Must Have
But the then
And the when has gone from here
And you are now breathless

She Delivered That You Wanted

She delivered that you wanted
You still were not happy
After all that taunting
Nothing to add to be sappy
You gave her what she asked
One child
And one to add
She asked you for relief
You looked at her
"How sad"
She questioned
You stated
I'd like to include one more
She looked at you
If serious,
A fool
For sure

What Did You Say

You said that
I would not amount to anything
Whatever I did
Would always be nothing
Recall
Recall 1
What Did You Say
She Said
When you said
She was nothing
Not knowing
She was about everything
And anything you could not stand
And you pushed her
Do you think?

' Life is so short. So live like you feel you have to!'

The Choice of Spoken Word

Never said my words have to be spoken
Always nice if they are read
I am not one out to gain a profit
And it is okay if I remain the way I am
But if my words touch one life
That is grand
I am not one to go crazy over stars
I have always said that and remain to say so
So I won't cry won't die if my words
Go unheard
For I have a voice where I am
Proud of what I am
Proud of the rocks I stumbled on
To get where I am
And if you should think
That I am nothing
If you should think
I am less than encouraged
If you should think
I am not working to your plan
Please remember
That I am who I am

For Brianna in her Confusion

All that she said
Was she wanted to be your all
If you didn't understand
You would watch her heart fall
She wants to be your everything
But she is afraid of what she has stumbled upon
She wants to be your wife
But she is afraid to move
Move with the unseen
The unknown life
This is for Brianna in her confusion
For the daughter she wants to have for you
This is for Brianna with intrusion
And the pain she sweeps away for you
She does not want you to be a secret
She wants you to be her being
She is afraid of the physical and mental
The abuse she could not live
For the grains of Brianna
She stands afraid
For she could not live
If they did not move with her
Through the door
Stay, Never go
Let the mind reconstruct
Let the heart know the truth
So that she comes solely to you
For Brianna is in love

Leave Me Alone

Leave me alone
I am poison
And everything
You wished me
Not to be
Did you not hear?
Leave me alone
I am poison
And everything
You wished
Not to see
Too complicated
High Maintenance
No Instructions
Nothing special
About me
I said High debt
I said many pains
Nothing will
Come from me
So why are you
Still staring at me
You say
You like spontaneity
You like the hell
I bring
You don't care about
Money
You are lying see
I say you won't want
Me in the morning

You won't need me the next night
So leave me alone
Go away
And I won't have
To put up this fight

You Can Be

You can be the circle
In my square
Let it be
Let it be
You can be the circle in my square
For we all know circumference
Can exceed that which compared
But I prefer square footage
In my despair
Now I can be your square in your circle
Covering even more than before

You Can't Do That For All

You can't please everyone
All the time
Don't get me wrong
There will always be someone
Pulling you in negative means
With sin on their bone
But don't let them tell you
That you can't succeed
That you can't do it alone
That you will have to give in
To the dirt near the stone
You can do everything you want
For you
But you can't do that for all

Vegetation

The vegetation inspired me
For there was not much
To live on there
Not much existing

A large peak stood ahead
And all that was alive
Was atop
I want to live and reach
The top
That's not much I'm asking
Just to climb and touch success
Success of the living vegetation

Beautiful bright skyline
Will engulf me
Will carry all the sweetness
Will lead me away
Blow winds to knock me down
To the vegetation of little existence
I will not live
For there's nothing to feed on
I will not give
For it is not success

Rains came down
Nourished the vegetation
Made it even more beautiful
To be consumed
To keep an eye
On the peak it lived

In the valley
Where I stood
Looking at success
I knew if I kept climbing
I would meet progress

By the hand
It would take me
And in so
It did
Giving me vegetation
Of the peak
To feed on
And live
Henceforth,
I have found success
And another wind came
Lower vegetation
I lived on
Once more

| 1991 |

Now You Wish

Now you wish
You had said yes
To what I asked
What I had wishes for
As you sit around
Watching me
Walk out of your life's door

Dreams of me
From day one to five hundred forty-four
You knew all along
That there was
Something unique
To be found in me
I was the one
To set you free
Of your little illiberal
Love live world

Your wishes of immaturity
Wishes of wanting to be with me
It's in your eyes
You see he with me
Eyes that cry
And reach for me
Love that dares not
To be set free
The qualities
That say neither
You or me

Desires come through you
See
Teach you
I must from words of you in me

I see your eyes
That watch me kiss
Wishing you were there again
I see your look of sadness
That speaks for itself
And says the vine
You were pricked
You bled
You thought
You said
I'll need a horse and armor
To charge next time

Untrue has
Tasted the taste
Of the bitter grape
That has grown old
With age
That will not let
Another charge
Without a soldier at hand

This is all
Because you stare at me
All because you
Wish the wishes of your destiny
To be with the one
To be the one
To not touch the vine
To be pricked again
Still you watch
You will learn
Now you wish
You had said yes

You Don't Understand

How can I love you?
When you treat him so bad
When you play the games you do
When you lie as you do
How can I love you?

I don't think you understand
For that is my brother
My Father
My Uncle
My son
How can I love you?
How can I say we are one?

When you don't see him
As you could see me
If you have no objective
For unity
If you stereotype
And run your satire
By the water cooler
And despise the color
Of your coffee
Untouched by cream or sugar,
Honey

You don't understand
See you can't love me
For you
Don't comprehend me
And your mocha twist coffee
Is just bland

The Sister's Message

She said I found your number
In my male friend's pocket
I'll call back later
Perhaps you dropped it
Per chance he picked it up
To dispose of

I awaited the call
And in return
I said
Sister's Message
Sister's Message
For your head

I met your friend
Last night
With no disclosure of
Relationship did he

In retaliation
She informed me
We are engaged you see
 I hung up ever so politely

It was a new catch
To let back to sea
For respect
Of a sister's message
And my lack
Of desire
Of sharing those
Before me

Don't You Dare

Don't you dare refer to me
As a soccer mom
Too eccentric for that
I am not a cc
Driving in a compact
I prefer a Hummer
And in truth
A great deal of variety
I prefer to shop on line
Than to walk the mall
Or boutique
And when you think I like to do
The things you do
Come again
And never compare

What About Your Mother

She said you show me no respect
You show me all that ignorance knows
And you will never know that I can be
So much more
Think about your mother I said
What about your mother we said

Did your father treat her like cattle?
Did your father tell you that was all women
Are good for?
When you sit behind your corporate desk
Is that all you can think when you have
A young woman
Behind closed doors
Shame on you
Think about your mother I said
What about your mother we said

For if you throw it across mainstream
Dirty and sleazy
We know what you think in your mind
So when you take pen to pad
And think it's just for fun
Think anew
There is a lesson for you to be had
Think truly if women were to exploit men
For that's all in good fun
But it's a man's world you said
Come now
Think anew
See yourself in your skivvies
Children don't look
Erect
Walking in nothing but such
In a public environment

Think correct
Think yourself pictured on a couch
Tongue hanging
Dripping wet
As you watch a female fully dressed walk by
Come correct
Now what about your mother
Sitting to watch you instead

I'm Tired

I'm tired of hearing
About someone else's kids
Every time I call you
I just want one conversation
Where you hear me through

Lord I think I have a sister
Just once in my life
I would like to have
One conversation with my
Primary Caregiver

I'm tired of hearing
About the nothingness air
I know you don't care
Seems like nothing I can do
Will ever be right for you
I can work as hard
To make the world see me through
And nothing of you
One recognition
By my primary caregiver

Lord I think I have a girlfriend
Just once in my life
I would like to know
Where you think
Your mind will go
And that fictitious lie you reared
To send me back thirty something years
Will never be forgiven
And I'm tired of my sensibility
Having to deal with your nonsense

My Savior

The thought came to my mind
You came to rescue me
From misery
Whether woman or man
You came to save
As you knew what
You were doing
Lover or friend
Enemy in the end

If you pushed too much
You were my Savior
My generator
Regulator
You became a source
Of provision
Non-living
Or cardiac rhythmic
You gave me sensibility of security
Security is all I asked
To believe

A fear of something grew
You took the time to listen
Showed a closeness
That we shared
If you were instrument
Or song
You were a book of hypocrisy
You did not wrong me
Savior of security
Was all I need
To believe

There You Go Again

I tried my best
You pushed me back
You opened your mouth
Said everything
And nothing at the same time
There you go again

Here I am trying to accept you
Incorporating you
Your soul
Your ethics
Your life
Into mine
And then you said the typical
Which was the erratic and
There you go again

Killing everything we had
And nothing we gained

And She Never Stays Still

She Never Stays Still for A Sunday evening
Always running as for the end of her life
No never sat still for a Monday morning
Even said no when he said
I want you for my wife

Everything she did was a portion here
A portion there
All because she wanted not to say
She did all she wanted to in life
And the easels they fell
The stories remained untold
The poetry would not tell
All the things to unfold
Everything unsold
And she never stays still
Until she met them
The beautiful children of her life

No No, Don't Address Me

No No Perhaps you thought
That I was your normal
Percentage what
slop?
Slop I am not
And I don't want to be approached
With what you got
Understand I'll stay poor
Understand the doors can stay closed
No No my mother raised me right
I had a mother unlike the kind
You are accustomed of being around
I have enough common sense to know better
And I don't want to have my child
In that environment
No No, don't address me
I said like that
Don't and we will be fine and free
And you will be oblivious to me

Nice Girls

No please don't misunderstand me
Think I am fooling you
Think I am arrogant
Think I am ignorant
Think I am some foolish girl
With foolish ways
I am much better than that
And so are you

I think you may want to understand
This too
Not that I don't like you
Seen you around
And find that your electrical stimulants
Are sublime
But we can do best
Not to make fools of ourselves
And put it down this way

Because the nice girls
Will let you know it this way
See if I am going to respect you
As you should respect me
No need to dance and prance in my life
And know nothing of me
Going to put it on the line
In due time
Because the nice girls tell you this way
And I say my no
Means no
And I can assure you that you won't hear yes
And I am looking at you
Seeing you
And wondering who thought to raise you best

Most likely I am not talking to you and you and you
But see the nice girls tell you this way
Maybe another day
Or should I be rude and raunchy that way
Not me
Should I be crude and laugh in your face?
You tried
And nice girls put it down this way
But see like you if you cross me
Nice girls will play the games you play
And I hate for people to see me this way
And I don't want to strain your look of dismay
And remember it goes both ways
Like the nice girls that put it down this way
Now Good day

Untitled

Don't do any drugs
Never will
Music is the best sensational high
Creating my own work is a natural high
I don't need any external stimulus
Unless it is love
And the strength found in it
Love in my mirror
Love of my family
Love of my significant other
Love in a God that knows not
Favoritism
And delivers love unconditionally

Don't Worry

Don't worry if it is precise
If you slipped on ice
Don't worry this time
Next time
It will all be fine

Don't worry if you made an error
Some call a blemish
Then you made that same error
Over and over again
Okay too much
Next time
Will be your final time
It's where you drew the line
Don't worry

Don't worry about
Being true to others
Be sure of yourself
And trust your actions
Know as an adult that you are
Far different than you were before
And that much more to be
For what will be in store
Don't worry
Don't worry

I Could

I could see myself
Jumping in your arms
Smiling as I use to
Waiting for your touch

These are the feelings
Coming from my heart
Shall I leave the man I love
For the man I have grown to love
All for the feeling again
Then I would have the one I love
Sitting alone
Picking up pieces
That were ours
As the one
I have doing now

There were strong faults
Things to make me mad
Those that made me sad
Times I was glad
These things still exist
With the one I love
And that not fulfilled
I say we all go about
That round-a-bout
Repeating feelings we had before
Repeat again
Repeat again
Or is it that we leave them behind

Should I smile with the one I love
As I had the one I loved
Or will the smile be as worn as the past day
For the one I have

Hurt me
And the one I love will do the same

There's just some secret power
That the one I have loved before
Holds over me
One that the one I do love can't
Fight or compete

Future tells me
To believe
The one I love will know the feelings
Of whom I loved
Will the one I love leave
As the one I have had

You are Untrue

You are untrue
If you say your convictions
Were not 'SOMA'
Some Of the Most Adolescence

You would be untrue
To say that a lot of that has not happened to you
You would be untrue
To point the finger
At someone needing the ear
And you would be untrue to be that much better
With your lies so unfair

Take your mirror and judge your reflection
And remember your penalty
For the mirror you use
So shiny and fine
Will be the mirror
You return to me

This Loving Thing

My Warranty

I promised you the day I met you
That I came with Warranty
Truly your satisfaction guarantee
With this thing
I call your warranty

09/23/09

I just wanted to let you know
It took a lot in me to tell you no
No to our past
No to our present
No to our future
How could I let it go
Baby I let it go
Because I love you so

You Can't Take It

You can't take it from me
For my pallet is Italian
With a dash of Mexican
My grandmother cooked
Food of soul
While my body
Danced the meringue
And salsa with stride

My soul reaches for the
Indian in my arteries
My heart cries for the Adrinka
Ethiopian, Aztec in my grandfather's ventricles
And at night as I sleep
I see the English, Irishman
Who called himself
My great great great
….and Francis the Narcisus
how true he may have beat some
But oh how he loved mine so
…enough to Father seven or nine
My grandmother says Samuel
 And you can't take it
Because it's hidden
And the soul at stake
Stays driven
For what is veined
Is the same

We Can Say

We can say that we know love
And be not a part of it
We can say we have fallen in love
And be far away
Than aware in it
For if we are in love
If we see love
If we know love
We know more than the meaning
We have become
Familiar with a way of life

The Reptile

The reptile
The serpent nearing the bow
I hope it shows you the love
That you deserve
It is not a painful one
Or one to give great direction
Just a whisper in your ear
To show affection
I hope you won't feel
Constriction
Not a boa
Not a killer
I hope you feel the love
That eludes from my heart
To you
For truly I am not a serpent
But a cuddly bear unwinding
They say 200 poems
They say   _words
They say many of pages
With varying flavors
This reptile
This snake
Does not come with venom
And attempts not to depreciate

Do You Remember

Do you remember
That our fabrics are the same
Our techniques seem to mirror each other
But you say I don't want to go there
Again
Do you remember
Our caramels our sun touched dews
Our folds reflecting the same hue
But you say that is not where you
Wish to return
And when you look at me
Your eyes burn
Not wanting to ever remember
The Moor of civilization
That brushed your way

That Is Not Cute

That Is Not Cute

They say in other countries
We like it a lot
We have no regard
For which is sacred
In our hearts
They say we move
From one topic to this
Not even paying attention
To how it,
We should regard
      That is not cute
And I am beginning to believe
That they are right
Beginning to believe
That we can't put up a fight
Against what they say
Because they say we
Freelance sex that way

They say in other countries
We like it a lot
We have excess on our tables
And hold stress as an appetizer
So that when we get to main course
We shovel for a man buried alive
As we promptly kiss the pillow for
A dream of cellulose
To wake in the morning
Overstuffed with a ten pound roast
That is not cute
And I am beginning to believe
That they are right
I am
Beginning to believe

That we can't put up a fight
Against what they say
Because they say we
Devour food that way
They say

They say we are selfish
We only think of us
We only think of what we want
And care not of what
It takes to get there
The forefather founding way
The Darwinian Survival Fit Domain
        That is not cute
And I am beginning to believe
That they are right
I am
Beginning to believe
That we can't put up a fight
Against what they say
Because they say we
Show ignorance that way
They say

How I Appreciate

How I appreciate your values
Your desire
Your drive
Truly I strive to be like you
Have a goal like you
Maintain life as you do
Once you have stumbled
Across your opportunity
Come true

Here is to the dreams
The dreams that you strive to achieve
Here is to the dedication
The long hours you work
To do what you do

This is for the immigrants
That come here with little
And work so hard to make a lot
Sometimes I forget that which I came
And realize how for granted
I take things I have not
For those that work
More than twelve hours a day to survive
And for my own who works twice as many
That I can keep what I live alive
For I, who works four to five jobs within one day
And for those that just realized the amount of times
Within eight hours they complained
This is how I appreciate the hard working people
In particular those that thrive honestly
…and this I knew then
Before it came

Untitled

Little _boys and girls singing grown up lyrics
That is not cute
I said Mature adolescence
Eighteen and rising
That is not cute
Children exploited
Their little voices
And I hate to see them sing a song
Too old for their years

Did you hear
Everyone will misconstrue
A public font
Labeled to who?
They say take it to your diary
Not good enough for the world to see
What about Emily
Heard she was talking Moorishly
Not everything made much sense
Even in divine defense
And they say
Nothing cute about that
What all does it mean

City Nights, City Lights

Moses

He led my feelings from the bondage
Of spiritual enslavement
Made the cobwebs part
Like the biblical did the sea
Led me to the promised land
Yet a dream
He couldn't fulfill for me

Beautiful curls of his mother land
Pure courageousness of his father's hand
Intellect I see
For he's abiding
Kindness no man could affect

Bring down my guidelines
From Mount Studio's peak
I will abdicate myself to the most High
For what you want in me

I am grateful
For my love prophet
Moses
For it will be told
From only you and God
What your future holds
And if you don't find
What you don't see
In her
Anymore
In me
But then reality took its course
For me to see
It was Bleak

Someone paid me

Someone paid me
All of that money
All of it to party
And I still can't find
Anything significant

I am grown
Past my thirties
Setting the example
For my kids
Kids let's go
Learn our abcs
And party

Someone paid me
All of that money
All of it to party
Party with them

I am grown
Past my thirties
Walking in the skimpy dresses
And nothing to think

Someone paid them
All of that money
All of that money
To have minds on a brink

City Nights, City Lights

Am I old enough for this?
Shh Shh!
From the street
To the mist
Walking up and down
Well lit stairs
From my heals to my
Curls
Shh Shh!
No one needs to know
In the city nights
The city lights
The East Orange scene
Those that I dream
Arriving late
But early in the morning
Warm up the grill
With the bacon and eggs
Comin' to the diner
About 5:48
The city nights
City Lights
Shh Shh!
My girlfriend
Said she'll
Be doing it till
She dies
But my o my
The time flies
And
The City Nights
The city lights
Are no longer for me
Even at the age of eighteen

Ambrosial

Multi disclosure
The leaves will be Ambrosial
She will ask all
Remember me

Semi-confusion
They'll say she's an illusion
And to her accounts
For her they'll weep

Half hearted arousal
They'll want the waves
To persuade them
From her tips

Benz she's driving
Material things she's parking
Commands that be in her garage'
Leaking as it seems
To them
Mirage is what it will be

From her roots
They'll scream
Wanting a taste of the cream
What cream of the crop
What say we

Mega-blessed Ambrosial
Say you wish to know her
Your only dream
Is to be a part of the sands

| 1991 |

That Part of My Life

It's the other part of my life
That which calls for me
To be of dark locks
Which causes me to enforce vogue
Sweet guidelines
Delicate etiquette
Of which some men do
Look and say
To touch would be ooh

That other part of my life
Which causes me to travel
From one destination betwixt an
Extraneous point of wishing
There was no return to base

That part of my life
I like to live
Of which mixes and bass capture me
And captivate the blackness
And I see a future for this
I see a future in this
Though others have told me
To rid of it

It's that other part of my life
Where the men I love, live
Of my life
Is that other part
That part of my life where I say
I live and love
And away too long
I too will miss you
For it keeps you going
It's how we do

| 1991 |

Perfect Man

Why are you the perfect man?
Why have you been made to be?
You are the perfect man
Perfect time
Perfect tag
Perfect line
Then when the world falls down
Rises and nothing is to be out of place
Though you
The one of perfection
Shows things that the world
Would consider
Out of space
Though you
The one of perfection
Shows things considered
Rejection
You still turn out to be
The best
Never seemed to be put to test
For you will be Czar
And nothing will be at wrong with you
Our normal lives
We see not in you
So we drift away
Knowing there is
Nothing we can do
To get to the perfect man
To live in the life of such
To do as much as hear a line
From the perfect man
In you,
I find

| 1991 |

Virgo Man

Birth came and he was a Virgo Man
Their man
Due to pacification of that particular drive
As my man
You will see differently
For we are compatible
And argue for the joy of it

Abandon the Capricorn
You couldn't
One would always have to wonder
About the other
However
Not daily

I see you sitting
The paper in front
Reading your horoscope
To see what it will direct
It tells you continuously
A Capricorn woman
Will hold fine for you
This is not an untruth

Will you see a future?
Virgo Man
Will you see it with the Capricorn woman?
Or will you let the fuse drive through
To your innermost being
Before two years
Of your promise of marriage
Will you decide on the right decision?
No knowledge
Of any provision

For you know in me
You can confide
Though you are the little boy
Who plays with the little girl?
By the city lights

Hold her chin
The Capricorn's
Carry your water well
Keep your eye
For the future
And let the Virgo's love
Prevail
…but you leave trails

| 1991 |

You Have Your Eye On It

You have your eye on it
Get it off
You think you can have it now
No No No No
You have one eye open
The other shut
You see the truth of your bad luck
You think you can have it back
No No No No
You think your chances
Are far from none at all
Well
I've my mind on that
And I've to tell you
The truth of the songs
I sung when you did me wrong
When I stood strong
When you weren't around
To be that I needed
When you knew all along
You had a gem
Then you decided you would
Taint it
No No No
No No No
All that I should have told you then
No No No
No No No

Now read the lines from my pen
All I want is my three hundred fifty
With one thousand dollars of interest
Don't want your love anymore
And for that
I've even the score
And remain without
Your companionship

Desire of Love

Every time they appear
They have a notion to disappear
Reappearing with images of past time

Different traits
They may carry
All to fall away and marry
The ways of desiring love
Desire of Love
Not above
Leads them to Pandemonium

The walls fell
For they heard me cry
And attempted to entrap me
In the Emperor's domain

Every time the appear
They appear in such a gorgeous manner
So as one can not keep their mind off of them

The Emperor controls them
And commands them
To come forth and entrap one
To ensnare
That victim is naïve
To the situation
That victim
I do not dare to be
For the desire of love
Is not where I dwell
It will end in hell

Every time they appear
Everything seems beautiful in one's life
They'll toil with the heart

Giving the notion of disappearance
Reappearing
Bringing forth images of past time
Re-assuring the victim
I'll be her
Everything is fine

I once victim
Have re-arranged my life
So that the desire of love
Will never carry me
Away a second time

| 1991 |

In and out of their lives
It goes
Seas of seasons
Winds of storms
And they know
What it beholds

Many a seasons
Of different reasons
Lovers come and they've gone
For they know
In this point of time
Loving here
What was
Is far behind
And won't be told
I'm to scold

| 1991 |

She said
I broke up with him today
Though I want him
For his call again
His eyes
His frame
That which I can't explain
And here is where
It was done well
That other one knew
All about him too well
And how it failed
I said…..
You little witch
Jezebel

Well

The echoes of pain
Once again in repeat
What was it I allowed
You to take from me
For I was a fool
As a young one I was
Well it ran dry
The rivers they shook
Life looked back at me
And wrote a new book
Told me I am too old
To be dancing that dance
And love was not true
For me to know your hand
Well it ran dry
And my heart pained me still
Lord knows I'm begging
I'm getting ill
Hoping you turn the other way
And realize I no longer
Live in those days
But I have and was
And never will again be
Yours

Didn't You Think

Didn't you think
I loved you
Held you
Stood by your side
Supported your wishes and whims
Well your thought was good
And you presumed you would
Saw that you could
And when you were gone
You didn't think
Of what you were in

Illusion

Can't Live Hidden

Do you want to know?
Really know why I can't live hidden
Well did you find out?
Did you see how blunt
Things can be about me
Yes I fell down like that
I am not perfect
Baby went boom
And wondered if it was worth it
Nose still bleeding
Waves of the wavelengths still reaching
And she wondered what the hell
Did she open
Damn Box of Pandora's dreams

Can't live hidden like this
For love knows no love
But that unconditional means
It seems

Illusion

Could she ever find that which
Was within her when she happened upon her
Well
Could she ever know what it was?
When you bumped into her
Thinking now illusion is what it is
Poor thing danced so hard
That her head tilted right
With all her might
She picked it up
Cried when you were crying
You didn't even know it
Was so angry
And Pained to see you
Hurts to even talk about it
Vowed then she would never fall again
Crazy fool she has pulled illusion in to hide her heart
Screaming your name out in her sleep
Knowing the heart was indifferent than
That she keeps
Normal everyday life in hidden screams
Illusions living in pain

Mimic

If we are going to do this
We might as well do it right
Let them know that we are
Brother, Sister, Father, Mother
Lover and Friend
See I am your sister
You are my brother
And you mimic my style
And I feed off yours
What is it that you have created
Amazed by that you have
Mimic me and I will respect you
Mimic me and I will accept you
Brother, Sister, Father, Mother
Lover and Friend
I don't need deep love
My heart
Will always mend
And my style was mimicked
My heart was mimicked
My mind was mimicked
And it wasn't all that bad
When my eyes were mimicked
My soul was mimicked
And my mate
Then left alone

Don't Think

There will be no love songs
Songs of love
Love other than unconditional
There will be no love songs
Songs of romance
The window that was left open
Was just closed
I don't think you understand
What happened to me these past few years
I hear it all
I feel it all
I see it all
But now there is a different part that is dead
What they didn't know
Was I was going through this
Ever since I was sixteen
Years ago how funny
With the call about basketball
Like a glacier
Like an iceberg
There is nothing left alive
To love other than how I have
I don't want that chamber opened
Don't want to go there
Don't want to know that
I am the cruelest
Individual that one could ever come across
I am worst than a storm
Worst than Black Ice

For that which is I
Taken from my life
I can't seem to smile
And never will again
As the electrical plug
Is far worse than the theory
And my adrenaline

For the Love of Illusion

I believeth that I shall detest myself
For living if I can't have you
If I shall live in idleness for the rest
Of my life
And not touch one
Air of your breath
I will be no more
In mere existence
For I think my soul will be ungrateful
And surely it will die
If I take one step
To journey without you
My sails will not open
My mast will not moil
For I will not be employed
If I am not in servitude to you
For one touch of you
Our souls to merge
Will be a true divinity
And without your permanence
For my exhalation
I could not see infinity

To The Sister She Never Had

She sat and looked
Smiled and mistook
All the things a sister could bring
Nothing but a thing
To misunderstand they were so
Far away
And so close as a touch of a hand
She said
I can't write you in right now
For if there ever was a script
To tell my open slips
You could only do justice
Of me
Novel Two Book Four
She closed her eyes
And closed the square box door
Her quill she picked
Off the sun stroked
Carpet floor
And said to the sister I should have
But never had
We are twins

Have You Ever Been
Mr. L. K. Soul Brother 4 Life

Have you ever been to Indonesia?
Just wondering
Have you been?
With all of it's splendor
That was then
It was then
The sun lit beaches
With moon lit kisses
Bombing then
How does it feel in Paradise?
For this is where I have dreamed of going
That was then
That was then
Now I don't know if that
Dream will ever come true
For my dreams of Indonesia
When
When
May never come true
Dear skies of blue
Could you tell me what it was like?
If you ever been

| 1990 |

In Love

Throw me a towel this time
I said for this time
I want You to
Throw me a towel
For it will be
If I am bound then be it for love
Let me hold a part of you near
For I have fallen in love
Fallen in love
With something I can't have

I beg of you to
Get that towel soaking wet
And slap my memories away
Slap them and make me think
Nothing but of you
Let me know nothing but you
And when it is all done
And I have kissed the towel
You have thrown
Say that I am yours
And no longer a drone

Damaged
(For Illusion)

I can repair what I turned you into
I can change you to be what you should be
I can heal your every wound
But you are damaged
I can sit back and laugh at you
As the others have before
I'm sizing you up for an easy kill
Listen to the words even more
Track 98
Track 87
Track 02
I never wanted you
Never needed you
You come a dime
You come a dozen
And your damaged goods
I want no more
Coming in for the kill
Coming in for the kill
Slapped love down on the floor
Your damaged goods
I want no more

Disposition

His call to her seemed to any other
That of irrelevance
Neither his mind or soul
Could make sense of it
All he knew at times
Was that a disposition
He was seeking
That until her voice was heard
There would be no end to reach
There would be no end of reaching

Her love for him
Were of chances slim
Though he figured constantly
Searching
The love in her would be tried

Sitting in his room
Asking why
I need to know why
He puts himself in the disposition

Venus come through to mend his brain
Mauberley labeled him psychotic

Love is like the sod
Could it fault
Could it rise
All I see
Is disposition
In his eye

| 1991 |

Not One Night With You

I don't want one night with you
Your whispers
Far from true
I want always
I want today
I want tomorrow
I want now
I'd give my life
And fire again
To touch my love
With you
This time
I won't say no
No one night
It's what I'm
Afraid of
Forever and
Always
I dream of
We both feel
The same way
I beg of you
To sing all things slow
As if you
Were upon my smile
In moonlight's glow
It sounds better
That way
And I want to say
Always
Today
Tomorrow
Now
I'd give my life

And fire again
To hold my love
With you
And never
Let it go

Firestarter - Holy Spirit

When you handed it to me
Didn't know
Didn't know
What I was to see
Now I know you have
Delivered the message to me
I was born with it you tried to explain
Maternal instinct
Was to blame it on
The unexplained
And that was because
I was born with the gift to be
Beyond formal
And now I sit with it in hand
Firestarter is screaming
How grand

I Don't Know You

I don't know you
Came from the lips
I don't know you
Pressing to kill the slip
I don't recall
Ever meeting you
Our acquaintance never was true
So I advise you
If you think to know of
What was and is
For the difference
You will see
Anything in correlation
You know not what you see
You know not what was she
You know not what you think
For the person and you
Are not in sync

Can't You See

Can't you see
What I am doing
Emerging with you
A oneness with you
This is absurd
Is what I've not heard
What I see
Is what I stay blind to
Loving where
Loving who
I won't allow you
This to be the death of me
The trick is
What you write
Will be your life
Thing is I always
Seem to let the old die
And come back
Again

The Eclectic

My Portions

My portions are much smaller
I am pushing away
Pushing away
You said Americans can not eat that way
I am listening to you
Listening to you
You say Americans do not care
About what we do
I am pushing away
Pushing away
So I can hear what you say
My portions are much smaller
I am going to change my ways

This is To My Brothers

This it to my brothers
In the 'gheadow'
Whom I never forgot
In the first place
The crazy innocence
The times we were blind
To who you were
Who you are
People first
Our brothers second

This one is for Candy
Who gave me her best
When she wanted to give less
Thank You

This is for the open hydrants
That some longed to touch
And for the brothers that worked
For the police department
And kindly opened them so

This is for waking on Saturday
And swinging to Santana
All day
This is for the love of East Trenton
And my Hispanic sisters
The mothers of my Hispanic brothers
Lovingly

The Eclectic

You will never hear me
Speak a word so eclectically
For I do not know all of these languages
But it's time I learned to pick up a few
So Eclectic
So vital
So much of necessity

You stare at the eclectic eye
In the eclectic time
Of our defaced minds
And perhaps it is time we become
Multi linguist
To understand the twist and turns
Of our society
Ever so eclectic
Eclectically

What good is a book
If it does not entertain
Many times I sit to understand
The unexplained
If you want to keep the interest
You have to pick up a new trick for the trade
Trade of mind for the conscious dime
So I bring forth
Reciprocation
The art of same
I bring in continuity with fixation to blame
I leave the dots for you to connect
To see what poem matches which
I even leave one hidden
As I comprise another with duo twist
And I hope with the concepts
You see the art unfold
For nothing is impossible
Your intrigue
As good as GOLD

Thank you for allowing me to greet you.
Thank you for allowing me to be in your mental presence.
Thank you for your words of discouragement
And those of encouragement
For your frowns
For the downs
The highs
The lows
And for those that know
I thank God for my gift
And the family that allows me to share
Until another rhyme......NMR

Nicci (Kneechi) Carpone–

If you have enjoyed this title, you may also enjoy:

"Soul of Mature Adolescence" Nikki M. Robinson-Williams
"Hemorrhage in My Head"   NMR

Printed in the United States
by Baker & Taylor Publisher Services